Steps in Leadership

Huw Thomas

C 02 0382222

 David Fulton Publishers

David Fulton Publishers Ltd
The Chiswick Centre, 414 Chiswick High Road, London W4 5TF

www.fultonpublishers.co.uk

First published in Great Britain in 2006 by David Fulton Publishers

10 9 8 7 6 5 4 3 2 1

David Fulton Publishers is a division of Granada Learning Limited.

British Library Cataloguing in Publication Data
A catalogue record for this book is available from the British Library.

ISBN: 1 84312 434 3

ISBN-13: 978 1 84312 434 4

Typeset by RefineCatch Limited, Bungay, Suffolk
Printed and bound in Great Britain

Foreword

No matter what responsibilities you carried as a deputy, or an assistant head, or a faculty leader, headship takes you into a whole new world. It comes home to you when you're suddenly aware that your short walk from the car park sends ripples all around the building – faces glimpsed at windows, someone dawdling through the entrance hall to be the first to say 'Good morning'. Then there's your chair, and the desk, and the awesome realisation that, in the end, everything that happens in this place is down to you.

It's not a feeling that ever goes away, either, because the role of headship changes all the time. The wise head knows that years of service aren't necessarily enough when it comes to keeping ahead of the game. Brand new challenges will appear all the time, right up to and into your final year in the job.

Help is at hand, of course, from fellow heads, advisers, parents, colleagues, the youngsters themselves. Importantly, though, there'll be times when you just want to read quietly and reflect upon the thoughts and ideas of others who've trodden the same road. That's where this series comes in. What you'll find in these short and focused books is, simply, 'words from the wise' – advice from people who know that your time is precious and are ready to link arms with you and take you, metaphorically, to one side and say, 'Look, this is something I know quite a bit about. Let me run you through a few things that work pretty well. Then, my friend, it's up to you.'

I visit many schools in researching the articles I write, and I'm privileged to see excellent things happening as teams of keen professionals respond to the needs of today's youngsters.

Some schools, though, stand out because they have a particular atmosphere that's not easy to define. Yes, the children are well behaved, the classes are purposeful (that's more common than some critics would have us believe) but there's something beyond that – a feeling that the whole place is somehow comfortably at ease with itself. As I talk to youngsters and staff in a school like that, I start to pick up real quiet confidence that the day will go well, that problems can be solved and challenges turned into opportunities.

Show me a school like this, and I'll show you one that's not only well managed, but well led.

It's not easy to define leadership. For some it's almost a mystical business – Shackleton returning to Elephant Island and calling 'Are you all well?' to the crew who'd been kept alive for four months on a freezing beach by their faith in his return. Or Churchill, rallying the nation to arms with a promise of only 'Blood, sweat and tears'.

How can you put all that in a book and pass it on? It's a daunting task, surely?

Maybe it is. Huw Thomas, though, is well up to it. He's no mystic, either. As you read his book he convinces you that leadership, for him (and, you can be sure, for the teachers and other colleagues who have worked with him) is a quality that's not only capable of being defined, but lies within your grasp.

Huw's title, Steps in Leadership describes exactly how he approaches the task of passing on his considerable experience. In effect, he walks alongside the reader, retracing his own learning steps, sharing the ups and downs, the ideas that work and those that don't. You believe him because he's done it – not as what he calls a 'superhead', but as someone '… still stepping into the job, sometimes striding, sometimes toddling with a bit of faltering and the occasional mad dash'.

Someone, maybe, just like you.

A long time ago when I was a head, a young firebrand of a teacher – a union activist in the days when that meant rather more than it does today – told me that despite our differences, he was convinced that I had what he called, 'The right sort of vision for our children'.

To my regret, what I didn't have, in those days when no one was talking about leadership, let alone preparing heads for it, were the skills to realise that vision to the fullest extent. All I can say is that if I'd had Huw's book beside me then, helping me put my ideas into order, I'd have done the job that much better. I'd probably, too, have spent rather less time hiding under the duvet – which, Huw tells us, in his ever-reassuring way, is one of the things that leaders invariably do from time to time.

Gerald Haigh

Acknowledgements

Thanks to colleagues at two schools, Springfield and Emmaus, who supported my toddling into leadership. The advisers, officers and fellow head teachers of Sheffield LEA have provided excellent support in this area, for which I am grateful.

Thanks to Pip Wilson, youth work trainer, for permission to use the image on page 63.

Thanks also to my editor, Margaret Marriott, formerly of David Fulton Publishers, and Wendy Janes, my copy editor.

This book is dedicated to Kate, who encourages every step.

Step 1

Are you sure you've got the right book?

Don't get me wrong. Picking up a book on leadership and opening it – I'm impressed. But there's one problem.

You might want to read a book by someone else.

See, this one isn't one of those books written by a dynamic leader who single-handedly swept into a failing school, tackled the duff staff, inspired the no-hoper kids and transformed it into a success story with an orchestra playing a weepy finale.

It is written by a head teacher, after a chunk of years as a head and deputy. But I'm no superhead. I'm still stepping into the job, sometimes striding, sometimes toddling with a bit of faltering and the occasional mad dash!

It's called 'Steps in leadership' because I've just found a few stepping stones that matter a lot. And they work for me.

If you're still with me, the next few pages give six thoughts about leadership that inform the whole of this book. They're possibly the closest the book gets to a theory of leadership.

If you've gone for the other book I hope it's worth it (though it probably cost more than this one – we're very reasonable!).

■ Leadership is like being up a tree

I still love to climb trees, so maybe that's why I'm indebted to Stephen R. Covey for a clear image of the difference between leadership and management (Covey 1989: 101). He asks us to imagine a jungle scene.

The managers have organised the task of hacking a path through these trees, using machetes. There is a good system in place that includes procedures for sharpening machetes and keeping machete wielders hacking away. He writes: 'The leader is the one who climbs the tallest tree, surveys the entire situation, and yells "Wrong jungle!" '

He also notes that the hackers and their managers will often respond 'Shut up! We're making progress'.

And that's the main ingredient of leadership. It's the ability to ascend to that perspective and, from there, communicate with those engaged in a task. It does sometimes involve tough messages and having to talk from a viewpoint you feel no-one else shares.

It also involves the hard work of getting that perspective – taking time to 'climb the tree'. But the view is fascinating. Step 2 will look at how we handle that perspective without ending up sounding like a prat.

■ Leadership is like pushing a blob

Another image: Thomas Sergiovanni says we should 'Think amoeba' and describes school leadership as being like pushing a giant amoeba across a road (Sergiovanni 2001: 7). It slips off the curb and we know where we want to get it, but something blobs out in one direction, in another place it's looking a bit thin, it starts blobbing off at an angle: 'Mind, heart and hand become one as the leader "plays" the glob, relying on her or his nose for globbiness, and ability to discern and anticipate patterns of movement that emerge' (p.7).

I've read that description to a number of school leaders and it always meets with a 'Yes!'.

I think it's one reason why we end up frustrated. The job has a constant, nagging undercurrent of feeling we haven't achieved what we would have wished or expected by now. Blobs are odd things to move.

However, Sergiovanni mentions that 'nose for globbiness'. We get to know our schools and our staff. The chapters on coaching and teamwork that follow will delve into that area with a realism that we're into amoeba thinking.

Leadership involves hiding under the duvet

Fairly often, on Monday mornings I curl up under the duvet and say 'I don't want to come out'. Inadequacy and anxiety wash over me and I am genuinely too scared of my job to do it.

By 9.30 the feeling has often gone. It certainly diminishes as the day wears on.

But, at times, the job looks too big and I just get scared!

When I'm into the practicalities I can do it. It's worth keeping a clear link between the big job and its basic steps. In the chapters ahead the emphasis will be on practical application. We're 'theory light' here.

What I'd ask you to do is apply the stuff in these chapters to real situations. Think of some forthcoming staff meetings as you read the chapter on vision. Read the one on teamwork with your crowd in mind. It's written with them in mind.

Leadership is like Gene Hackman in an upside down boat

We're reflecting on leadership. One of the healthiest exercises at the outset of such a process is to list and think about the leaders we would and wouldn't follow. I can think of heads of department, head teachers, team leaders who have inspired me, and I need those images in my mind. I need to be asking: 'When they lead why would I follow?'

Personally, I go for Gene Hackman in that classic disaster movie *The Poseidon Adventure*. There came a moment when, after the boat had turned over, the passengers had to decide whether to stay put in the ballroom or follow the mad preacher through this dangerous wreck. A few followed, and I just love that scene where he persuades them that 'life' lies in the direction he is going.

In the section on leadership styles we will tease out the ways people lead and take some time looking at vital characteristics. Might come in useful on an upturned cruise ship, if nowhere else.

▦ Leadership is like telling stories

How do you tell them it's the wrong jungle? How do you present a vision of the right one? How do you map out the journey?

Leaders provide their staff with ways of understanding and perceiving, whether it be the stories we tell about the school or the images we use, we need to find ways of symbolising the school and its task.

So this book does take time to look at ideas. When we look at vision we will look at the thinking behind its presentation. When we look at teams we will look at some of the thinking that's gone into understanding the process by which they operate. We'll keep coming back to practicalities, but without that sort of thinking you will use the ideas and then dry up. Where it is included this more theoretical stuff is designed to kit you out with ways of shaping your own thinking.

▦ Leadership is great . . . just great!

Maybe I shouldn't say that. I mean, we're supposed to pull faces and look hassled. But the fact is, I get to shape the place that will shape the minds of thousands of people in their most formative years. I do it through working with a group of interesting, vibrant and fun people. And the best part is I'm still learning the job. Each year passes and it feels like I've gathered a bit more of the job to myself, taken a few more steps. Maybe we should allow ourselves to feel great about this job a bit more often.

OK, that's the closest you'll get to some grand theory. There might be one in one of the other books – but if you're still here, let's get on with the job.

Step 2

How can I do the 'vision' thing without sounding like a prat?

■ Feeling like a suit

Standing up and giving the 'vision' thing, that leaves me feeling a bit unsure of myself. The vision ain't the problem! I've got the ideas, I know what I'm wanting for the school.

It's trying to stand there and present it without feeling ridiculous. It's the anxiety that they are going to nod while thinking 'What the . . .?' It's the sense I might start sounding like a suit training sales reps. It's feeling like it's all a bit too flip charts and power pointed for me.

But the vision thing matters. The Ofsted findings concerning successful leadership and management took the results of inspections under the previous framework and turned them into the new framework. Top of the list came the need for: 'a clear vision, with a sense of purpose and high aspirations for the school, combined with a relentless focus on pupils' achievement' (Ofsted 2003: 7).

When teachers were surveyed to find out which image of leadership they considered effective, the highest scoring description was: 'Leadership means having a clear, personal vision of what you want to achieve' (Moos, Mahony and Reeves 1998: 63).

The vision thing matters because it makes the crucial difference between leading and managing. Remember Covey's jungle image in Chapter 1. The managers organise the hacking through the jungle – but to be a leader you need to be up the tree. Someone needs to have a sense of direction and bring that to the workplace. When it comes to moving in a direction, there are three vital elements to the journey.

Activity

Look at a staff list and ask:

- What is the significance of vision for this group at present?
- What experience have they had of this sort of thinking in the past?
- If I were to get them on board with my vision, what difference would that make to my school?

■ 1 Where are we going?

A leader is like a bus driver. If you jump on a bus you'll be asking this question. You want to know if it's taking you to Manchester Airport, and then on to Ibiza, or if it's headed for Cleethorpes.

But in a school we all know what direction we're going in, right? In general most of us will be able to trot out similar things we would like for our school: happy environment, achievement, discipline. Yet, if staff are to follow a lead it needs to offer something more specific in its design. Vision involves being clear about just where it is we are going.

Vision translates the glib into day-to-day reality

In promoting a vision the school leader has a chance to take the glib and standard goals, the sort of thing we trot out to please Ofsted or our interview panel, and translate them into the specifics of the school context. In sketching a vision, general goals like 'high achievement' become applied to specific schools in which there may be the challenge of high turnover or children with low baselines. A will to see achievement will translate in one way in these settings, and in a different way within a school that faces the equally challenging circumstance of high performing intake and parental pressure.

Vision guides decisions

When one of my parents asks to withdraw a child for a day so he can perform a Mexican dance at a reception for the new vice chancellor of her university, what guides me? This opportunity is at odds with his attendance in a day's lessons. I need some sense of what my school is about, to guide in such nitty gritty decisions.

Vision comes to bear in the nitty gritty of school life. Leadership can involve making hard decisions and sacrifices. These will usually be guided by a long-term perspective. If you had to choose between a quiet life and the need to tackle a colleague who was exhibiting poor performance then you face a tough choice. Shall I go for the quality of teaching or the will to maintain a happy workforce? It takes a long-term vision to guide that decision.

Vision promotes identity

A school leader should be able to present a vision for their specific school. One interesting question to ask in this regard is: 'How is your vision different to what the school down the road would say?' When I sit on your staff team listening to you rousing the group I'll be inspired if you can make it specific, because one of the motivating qualities of such a motivating call should be the sense that my job is unique, my context is unique and I'm led by someone who can see and explain that uniqueness. Otherwise I'll be tempted to think it's just some presentation you picked up in a management book.

Gaining the vision

If my vision matches the realities of my school then I'll sound less of a pratt when I'm explaining it. That sense of unique identity will rely in large part on the analysis a leader conducts of the context in which they are to give a lead. This will consist of four actions:

a. Analysing
Analysing data, such as previous Ofsted report, PANDA reports and any internal evaluative material is a start. Crucial in all this is the conversations had in the early stages of coming into leadership. Don't waste a moment, and remember most people like to talk about what they do and most conversations in this vein touch on frustrations within the job. These can be a useful point to probe and ask a little bit more – though take care with this, people want to be listened to, not mined!

Within the first 100 days of leadership there is a 'honeymoon period'.

Taffinder reminds us that 'many incoming leaders (CEOs, departmental managers, new sports coaches, even politicians taking new political office) have an extraordinary advantage in this regard'. During this period the 'insider-outsider' leader can 'get to know the enterprise in depth without suffering the constraints of being completely a part of it' (2000: 29). It's a time for asking, a period when you can say 'I'm making no changes at present, just finding out'. In school terms that roughly equates to a first term and feels about right as an estimate of how much time you spend on this 'honeymoon'.

This information seeking doesn't end after 100 days. Leadership requires an ongoing process of finding out and digging deeper. Leaders will occasionally set up little enquiries to gather and analyse information.

It is also important to have some clear conduits of information from the world beyond the school. Choose a few sources – things to read, such as the TES, briefings to prioritise and people to catch up with. Stick to these, they provide a necessary source of information that comes to you – and also through you to the staff team.

Vision questions

- What do I want to see in three years' time?
- Why choose that vision? Why is it important?
- If that's the destination, what would a mid-point look like?
- What are the distinctive words I could use to describe this vision?
- How will we know we are there?
- Where are we travelling from?
- What might prevent us reaching that destination?
- What would my first step be?

---

b. Reflecting

There are certain key questions we can ask ourselves and those in our leadership team as part of the hammering out of our vision. Following the questions Taffinder proposes (2000: 33) I've put together a list of questions that can structure the task of hammering out a vision. Taffinder suggests taking questions like these and writing a short story based on the answers. Howard Gardner, in his analysis of leaders, suggests that it is this sense of story that gives 'a dynamic perspective . . . a drama that unfolds over time, in which they – leader and followers – are the principal characters and heroes' (Gardner 1996: 14). It may seem odd, writing a story that couldn't be told for a few years, but in writing it down we both animate our vision and sharpen its focus.

c. Symbolising

So why does the vision thing sound pratty? Well I'm sure you, like me, have sat there as someone supposedly enters into a presentation with the aim that we, the audience, should catch a glimpse of the road ahead. They proceed to talk too much.

If I asked you to take the answers to the questions above, take the story you tell and turn it into a list of five words, what would they be? In my first year of first headship our school's list was monitoring, progress, objectives, stability and inclusion. These five words constituted our vision for our school. (Figure 2.1 shows the little card staff had as a preparation for Ofsted!)

You need to think hard about these words. Spend a bit of time with the thesaurus. When my staff were working on a mission statement for our school, a sentence to sum up what we were about, we started with an idea of 'promoting achievement' or 'fostering' it. The idea was picked apart and put together again, until a couple who were keen gardeners alighted on the word 'cultivate'. With its overtones of nature, growth and responsiveness, the task of 'cultivate achievement' became ours.

Thomas Sergiovanni talks about an idea called 'symbolic leadership' emphasising the leaders role in providing 'symbols that count and . . . help parents, students, teachers and others make sense of their world' (Sergiovanni 2001: 24). I worked with a head teacher who used the symbol of stability in a chaotic context, talking about the school door as a symbol of where the chaos ends. The door became a real symbol in that school of the point at which standards of behaviour were set and, as a new teacher, I could relate to that idea. I caught that vision. I heard these ideas communicated in a way that has powerfully connected the idea with the here and now, making it something worth striving for. This is what Sergiovanni means when he talks about 'leadership with ideas'. It's worth spending a bit of time identifying and symbolising those shared meanings.

Key messages to the Inspectors

During the inspection week we aim to highlight our grip on these things.

■ Monitoring	– used in development planning through subject reports – involved observation, scrutiny of work and planning
■ Progress	– use of assessment week target setting
■ Objectives	– clear planning and timetabling – we know what we are teaching and they are learning
■ Stability	– environment we create for turbulent admissions – clear discipiline policy
■ Inclusion	– range of ability – differentiation

Figure 2.1　Pre-inspection reminder

d. Clarifying

Whatever the vision that is starting to form, aim to keep it simple. If ideas are gooey, split them up into details. If they are too scattered and messy, try to find some sort of organising principle. I have a useful standard for how clear I've made things, close to hand in a primary school. It's this: could I explain it to an eleven-year-old – can you do that with your vision?

■ 2 How are we going to get there?

Back to the image of the bus driver, once we know the destination we still need to consider the different roads that can take us there and navigate a route. There is a real dynamic at work here – the route could follow a lot of varied twists and turns, we could set off cross country – who knows?

Coupled to the creative and diverting possibilities we need an ability to figure out the route we will take. There is a similar task to be followed in leadership. When presenting the vision and aims of a school we need

■ creative thinking about ways forward

■ credible presentation of the best route

■ strategic response along the way.

Creativity

The most direct road may not be the best one. There may be short cuts. Who says we have to get there quickly?

Creativity is an essential component of the leading journey. Innovative thinking requires leaders who adopt creative thinking – and, crucially, promote it within the staff team. In their work on creativity McLeod and Thomson outline a process of creativity in which two vital steps are the challenging of preconceptions, leading to 'looking at things with a fresh eye' (McLeod and Thomson 2002: 7). These are vital steps in a job where the constraints can seem overbearing. Funding can be poor, external directives can bear down and situations can seem insoluble. Creative thinking involves a simple refusal to be bound by one possibility and a determination to see further possibilities. I recall standing with one head teacher of an amalgamated school in her playground as she talked of a sports and arts facility she wanted on site. She outlined what it would look like, how it would run. A governor in our party pointed out her vision already sounded like tens of thousands of pounds worth of work in a school strapped for cash. 'That's not the problem', she responded, 'If we see what we need we'll then get the money'. She shifted the talk away from the one-way street of dried up funding – and two years on her school has a facility to be proud of, funded by a hefty grant.

Creative strategies supporting a vision

The long-term goal was improved punctuality. The problem was lateness. Statistics showed that 30 per cent of the school turned up late, some were very late. Printed below are some creativity strategies with the ways they were played out in the discussions that followed.

Creativity strategies	Conversations included exchanges like:
Say things in a different way: ■ try restating the problem ■ as things are said in discussion, repeat the idea while remoulding the sentence	'A third of the school is late' – 'So two thirds are punctual' 'A third of the school is late' was remoulded to 'School starts before a third of the kids get here'
Start from what you want and work backwards: ■ talk about the solution, what it would look like and you begin to talk about ways forward	'If everyone was on time what would it look like?' 'You'd go outside five minutes before the bell and everyone would be here' 'Maybe later on in this plan we should think about what we do in the first five minutes of the day' 'Imagine if they were unmissable'
Ask 'why?' and 'how?' questions	'Why do families arrive five minutes after the bell?' 'Why are they so close?' 'Why aren't they half an hour late?' 'How do things work if you are late?'
Let your mind wander	'What about the bell on the roof?' 'It worked for the Victorians' 'How could we replace it?' 'Think of the headlines – "Old bell solves new problem" – would a heritage trust be interested in backing that?'

Stories like that may seem simplistic, but I depend on them because they reinforce certain key elements of creativity. Volumes have been written on this subject but, for leading staff in pursuing a vision, there are some strategies that can be useful. To illustrate them I've used a specific school's problem and goal.

If creativity is to become an accepted means of finding new ways forward it needs to be encouraged within a staff team. Two ways of doing this include:

Asking for more
Conversations like the examples above happen when staff are encouraged to say more.

■ Ask for another one; when a problem is expressed, sometimes the first person to say a solution can be the only one unless someone says 'OK, thanks for that, jot it down and let's add some more' or 'That's a thought. Let's not fix on one just yet, until we've heard a few more'.

■ Don't dismiss an idea; a daft idea can stimulate a better one and every daft idea acknowledged sends a message to everyone in the room that the floor is open for ideas.

Gathering people
■ People are motivated by acknowledgement. A quick request: 'Can I borrow you and Alison at home time for five minutes? I need your thoughts', makes it clear we value our team member enough to ask. Roping staff into thinking things through generates a commitment to wider, creative thinking.

■ Don't forget to make a specific point of thanking people immediately after such help – and to do it by the next day, in earshot of others.

■ Don't always ask the same people – vary the list.

Remember: creativity comes from many sources and a wandering mind. A bloke called George de Mestral once got burrs on his trousers while out walking the dog. He went on to invent Velcro (so next time some five-year-old lets rip with the Velcro strap in assembly, blame George's dog!).

Credibility

When it comes to vision in education, credibility can be seen as the acknowledged capacity to navigate the way. That can be made harder by the constant change in the profession.

Teaching is a profession in a state of permanent revolution, constant change, often developed within the organisation but equally often landing on our desks from some external authority. As I write this, I am coming to the end of this year's action plan for my school – the tool we use to navigate the route we take to certain destinations. During the twelve-month life of this one plan we have been taken into an Education Action Zone, a pilot project for Key Stage 1 and a pilot leadership project.

How can we establish and maintain integrity in such a fluctuating context?

Look wider

The next big change is on the horizon, and the leader is the one who sees it coming. Maybe not in detail – (I'm writing this two weeks after the government promised to tell us how the next major pay reform would work, hoping and wondering if they'll ever get round to it before the dates when we have to implement it) – but we are the ones who read the education press, who maintain some on-line contacts that give us a 'heads up' on what lies down the road.

Mediate

Be the one to tell staff what lies ahead. If you read or hear of some initiative on the horizon mediate the information to staff. The final outcome may be radically different from what you presented as a possibility, but by being the one presenting first and second drafts of changes you maintain credibility as the navigator who can lead through them.

Adopt a strategic intent

Sting sang 'Let your soul be your pilot' – not a bad motto in turbulent situations. We can know our big intention, our significant vision – the soul of the school – and allow this to guide while also planning at the levels at which we can manage step by step.

Boisot (1995, quoted in Davies and Ellison 1999: 17) makes the useful distinction between 'strategic planning', something we can do when the turbulence is low, and 'strategic intent'. Whatever turbulence may disrupt the coming years it is possible to clarify intentions. In a turbulent situation, such as a school amalgamation, constant changes in a building programme may frustrate an understanding of when certain tasks can be done and who will be available to do them. Above such specifics there is the less frustratable intent: we will bring staff together to hatch a joint vision, we will have a single discipline structure in place to give children security from day one etc. Boisot's message is quite liberating – distinguish what you intend from what you can clearly plan. I think this gives something of an answer to the question about whether it is ever worth doing a three-year development plan. The answer is: yes, provided you see it as a set of intentions and don't tie years two and three down to such a degree they can be frustrated by the turbulence of the job.

Alternatively, an organisation 'operating in a regime of strategic intent can use a common vision to keep the behaviour of colleagues aligned with a common purpose'. Davies and Ellison comment that 'this is a very powerful way of linking futures thinking and strategy in order to provide direction and purpose for an organisation as it takes account of high levels of turbulence but maintains high levels of understanding of the core direction needed' (Davies and Ellison 1990: 16). The distinction is vital in maintaining credibility with staff. It's about saying 'Here's what I see us doing, here is the intention, and it stays there regardless of what turbulence does'. It says things like 'We need to see creativity in the majority of our lessons and even if creativity is outlawed tomorrow I'll still hold that up as a vision'.

Now we're really going cross country!

Don't shy away from inspiration

I do find it hard to say the big picture things without feeling like a wally. I hate this part of the job – but there are two things to bear in mind, a do and a don't.

Do write down the vision you want to present and present it to staff. Whatever your style is, flashing it in powerpoint across the screen or saying 'I believe this passionately but I still need to read it from my notes', it needs saying. Staff are looking for it.

Don't try doing it like someone else's vision. If someone else has a good idea, grab it. But the stuff you present under the banner of vision needs a bit of the personal touch.

Activity

Personalising vision – what's your metaphor?

Choose your metaphors from what interests you – football, cooking, DIY, marathon running . . . poker? Most passions in life can prove a rich source of image and language for the visions we want to propound. Don't be tied to ones used elsewhere – feel free to use your own. It will personalise the ideas even further.

If you feel comfortable talking about 'a long ball game' or a 'fallow season' then choose your image and use it where it fits.

Questions for reflection

- How is my vision specific to my school?
- Which five words would I use to symbolise my vision for my school?
- How do I gather information about the wider world of education?
- What about my background or experience motivates me to opt for my particular vision?

---

3 Communicating direction

Unless it's thoroughly communicated a vision will falter. It can result in the worst sort of disjointed relationships between leadership teams and staff. It can create isolated bullying head teachers and confused or demoralised staff.

Communication skills are the stuff of whole books – but here is a short list of the skills that support the communication of vision.

a. Plan beforehand

Effectively communicating vision is a must. Look at it with this sense of value and you'll at least run through the main points beforehand. If you're about to present a vision to your team, run through it beforehand with someone who will pick up any ambiguity or ask pertinent questions.

b. Talk to individuals

A group is a group of people. Make eye contact with them as you talk through things. Refer to individuals – if you've made the most of your first 100 days you'll be able to refer back to 'That conversation we had about creative arts' and other such background chats.

c. Break up the content

Organise what you have to say under clear headings. A lot of communicators recommend the use of three points (Holmes refers to the number three as 'a natural and poetical ingredient of conversation' (1999: 57)) however, it would be unwise to cut the vision to match the quota of points. The main recommendation is to structure what you have to say to around three to five headings.

d. Share visuals

A handout, an OHP, a powerpoint presentation – there are people who will follow what we say all the more for having it appear visually in front of them. It also assists you in making the presentation to be able to see the main thoughts that structure the whole thing.

e. Use clear language

Make clear statements of intention and distinguish these from questions. Avoid the unsure 'I thought it might be a good idea if we started a parents group'. It is either 'We can start a parents group', 'We will start a parents group' or 'I'd be interested to hear your views on a parents group'.

f. Pace your presentation

People will spend all day learning varied activities for teaching science, but vision-type presentations should be snappier. When it comes to inspiration it needs to be pacy to have impact. Longer sessions will dissolve into fluffiness or drag into tedium. Absolute maximum one to two hours presentation and discussion leaves it open for those who want to, to stick around for a longer chat, freeing everyone else.

g. Revisit

Beyond any initial presentation and crucial to the communication of a vision is the golden rule: revisit, revisit and revisit. Link it to other matters so it comes at the head of discussions on the initiatives that will stem from the vision. Wheedle it into conversations. Ask questions that link to it. Taffinder recalls how, in an industrial context, the head of a large pharmaceutical company once said on this subject: 'Communicate the essence time and time again, until you are sick of saying it. Even then, you probably haven't communicated it enough' (2000: 40).

Step 3

Different styles of leadership

Ever seen a bully at work?

Some years ago, when the pressure really came on our schools from performance tables and Ofsted, we also witnessed a spate of stories about management bullying.

Suddenly, head teachers had budgets, they were responsible for monitoring, the burdens of leadership were placed upon them. In some cases the pressure turned into hideous behaviour towards staff. I have a theory that this was due to a combined effect of cranking up the leadership role *without* a corresponding emphasis on enabling those leaders to reflect on how they, personally, did the leading.

Effective leadership requires an acute degree of self-awareness. This will include:

- knowing what sort of leader I am
- knowing how I lead differently depending on the situation
- knowing the sort of leader I want to be.

Facets of leadership

There are numerous lists and models presenting an image of educational leadership. The National Standards and the average person specification give some 'bread and butter' requirements, such as ability to manage a budget – or there are the bigger picture ones.

Activity

Before looking at my list, write your own. If you had to list five requirements for a good leader in education what would they be?

For the record, Table 3.1 shows the facets of leadership I look for and aspire to (and who knows, I may manage a couple of them, one day!).

■ Leadership styles

Table 3.1 could be described as an inventory of what leaders do.

However, each leader will approach the job in a different way, possessing their own style of leadership.

In an article written in 2000, Goleman summarises the findings of a research project undertaken by the Hay/McBer Group, drawing on a sample of 3,781 executives. Researchers managed to identify six distinct leadership styles.

Table 3.1   Facets of leadership

Visionary	■ a sense of vision
	■ seeing where we want to be in the future
	■ looking beyond the current picture
Organisational	■ a capacity to translate vision into planning and action
	■ making things happen
Personal	■ communicating vision
	■ motivating staff
	■ being sensitive to the individuals and the team as a whole
Educational	■ having a sound grasp of educational thinking
	■ keeping a grip on current changes in the profession
Symbolic	■ the leader 'makes meaning', focusing attention on what matters to the school
	■ symbolising this and representing it to others

The six vignettes in Table 3.2 provide portraits of the six styles of leadership. Each style is accompanied by the little phrase Goleman uses to describe it. A brief description, a note about research findings regarding its impact on the workplace climate and some significant points to note about the usefulness and difficulties of each style. It is worth noting Goleman's health warning throughout this section: 'Leaders with the best results do not rely on only one leadership style; they use most of them in a given week' (2000: 78).

Table 3.2   The six styles of leadership (after Goleman 2000)

	Coercive
In a phrase	'Do as I tell you'
Climate impact	Most negative of the six It limits employees' sense of flexibility – the freedom to innovate. Goleman describes their sense of responsibility evaporating, with (to quote) the words: 'I'm not going to help this bastard' (p. 82)
Description	This sort of leader gives orders and expects compliance. Goleman refers to the CEO who engages in a reign of terror.
The effects – this style . . .	■ is very damaging to morale ■ undermines the chance to motivate ■ has worked masterfully in crisis situations or when compliance is vital ■ is not to be relied on solely
Main use	Crisis situations where speedy or forceful decisions are the best way forward
	Authoritative
In a phrase	'Come with me'
Climate impact	The most effective leadership style, creating an effective working environment
Description	A style that 'sells' ideas, by showing a team of people how a proposed way forward accomplishes a goal they all share, so encouraging them to move in that direction

(continued)

Table 3.2 Continued

The effects – this style . . .	■ motivates staff by showing how their work fits the big picture ■ states the 'ends' of a vision, giving appropriate leeway to decide means ■ according to Goleman, does not work so well with experts in a field or peers more experienced. In a field like education where the constant change gives a knock to everyone's expertise over a period of five years I would question this ■ can struggle after initial ideas lose their excitement: needs to guard against new vision for the sake of it
Main use	Inspiring staff to attain a vision
	Affiliative
In a phrase	'People come first'
Climate impact	Very positive
Description	This style 'revolves around people – its proponents value individuals and their emotions more than tasks and goals'. It includes the giving of 'ample positive feedback' and creating of a 'sense of belonging' (p. 84).
The effects – this style . . .	■ places a big emphasis on building relationships ■ involves openness of emotion, including the leaders being open about their emotions ■ exclusive focus on praise can allow poor performance to go unnoticed
Main use	Supporting staff, in a 'club culture' where they feel emotionally connected to the school
	Democratic
In a phrase	'What do you think?'
Climate impact	Positive effect
Description	Employees are very much a part of the decision making process. This style involves 'spending time getting people's ideas and buy in' (p. 85).

The effects – this style . . .	■ drives up flexibility and responsibility
	■ results in the leader learning what would keep employees' morale high – though it's another matter whether the leader can then provide it
	■ can result in an endless schedule of meetings
	■ is ideal when the leader is uncertain and needs to gather ideas and opinions
Main use	Consulting and ascertaining the views of colleagues

Pacesetting

In a phrase	'Do as I do, now'
Climate impact	Negative effect
Description	This is leadership by example, outpacing everyone else at work. 'Leader sets extremely high performance standards and exemplifies them himself' (sic) (p. 86). Such a leader has little time for poor performers.
The effects – this style . . .	■ suits leaders who have guidelines in their head but do not state them clearly. In this style, people are expected to know what is required: 'If I have to tell you, you're the wrong person for the job'
	■ can work with highly skilled and motivated teams, who will try to catch up with the extra pace
	■ engages the school in a 'change marathon' (Fullan 2001: 37) in which a classic hero-Head is driving everyone forward without developing their capacity for and commitment to improvement
	■ should be used sparingly
Main use	Setting an example of the sort of professional conduct and activity expected of staff

(*continued*)

Table 3.2   Continued

	Coaching
In a phrase	'Try this'
Climate impact	Positive
Description	Time is invested in coaching staff, with the leader coaching staff on how to do their job. It involves enabling colleagues to evaluate and develop their performance.
The effects – this style . . .	■ is about developing others ■ says 'I'm investing in you' ■ involves giving plentiful instruction and feedback ■ is of little use where staff do not want to develop their skills and careers and makes little sense if employees are resistant to change
Main use	Developing the skills and careers of staff

At its simplest (in fact – at its over-simplified), if the display outside the classroom needs putting up, these styles would react with six different responses to the teacher concerned:

Coercive: 'Put that display up, now'

Authoritative: 'The reasons a display would be a good idea are . . .'

Affiliative: 'That's a lovely blank wall – well done!'

Democratic: 'Who votes for putting up a display?'

Pacesetting: 'I'll put the display up for you'

Coaching: 'I'll show you how to put the display up'

Activity

Over the course of the past week, think through times when you have drawn on the leadership styles described in Table 3.2.
Ask yourself what your dominant style has been.

■   Think of specific incidents, asking 'How would it have been different if I had adopted an alternative approach?'
■   Which of these styles could I cultivate further?

However, it's not as simple as asking these questions. The following four points are essential add-ons to this skim through the styles.

1   **There are dominant styles:** we all have dominant styles – the ones we tend to use more often than others or that break through our use of the others. We need to be aware of our own tendencies.

2   **Different situations need different styles:** each style has a time when it works best – even those with an overall negative effect on climate. When the school catches fire you don't vote on evacuation – you order it. 'Elements of different leadership styles must be learned and used in different situations' (Fullan 2001: 46). Knowing this can provide a framework for thinking about tasks ahead. It can be useful to look towards various discussions and situations in the coming week consider which styles will come into play in various situations – so I may expect to give clear dictates about ending playtimes promptly but may gauge opinions democratically about whether assembly should be shifted to after playtime.

3   **We need to use the range:** Gillen suggests a parallel between leaders who use one leadership style and a broken clock – 'right twice a day but, the rest of the time, it will be inaccurate to varying degrees' (2002: 146). Goleman suggests 'Leaders with the best results do not rely on only one leadership style; they use most of them in a given week' (Goleman 2000: 78). He goes on to add: 'Leaders who have mastered four or more – especially the authoritative, democratic, affiliative and coaching styles – have the best climate' (Goleman 2000: 87).

4   **Styles vary in their usefulness in 'implementation dips':** as organisations go through change they experience 'implementation dips' (Fullan 2001: 40) – dips in performance and confidence as the innovations present a challenge. Fullan comments 'pacesetters and coercers have no empathy for people undergoing implementation dips', whereas 'effective leaders have the right kinds of sensitivity to implementation' (Fullan 2001: 40).

■ Understanding authority

The exercise of authority is a vital and variable ingredient in the different leadership styles available to us.

The political philosopher, Hannah Arendt, saw any use of force or coercion as an abandonment of genuine authority, stating 'Where force is used, authority itself has failed' (Arendt 1954: 93). She stands alongside a succession of thinkers who want to distinguish between the use of power and the exercising of authority.

One way of getting your own thoughts together about these two concepts is to momentarily think how you would use these words – what examples of their use spring to mind? Can you move from these to some notion, not just of a definition, but of a difference between the two?

According to Jenkins, authority involves a triangular relationship, in which someone is able to exercise authority because the one subject to that authority can see that, by following the plan of action or suggestion proposed, they will attain a desired goal (Jenkins in Harris 1976: 36). This could be based on the track record or persuasive powers of the one exercising authority – but when it works, it garners the consensus of those subject to it.

Conversely, power is about force. If I exercise power I make you do something, maybe because your contract binds you to follow my instruction or because I'll get angry if you don't. Either way, it involves coercive force.

Clearly the ideal model of leadership is to be in a position to lead with authority, though there are times when power also has to be wielded. If someone wants unpaid leave the day before half term to catch a cheap flight and I say 'No', I can either use the power I have to say 'If you take a day off I'll discipline you', or I can explain why granting your request would bind me to grant the requests of others leading to competition to have days off the Friday before half terms and an impossible dilemma for the school.

One of the best pointers to handling this relationship well lies in the assertion of Thomas Sergiovanni that this is a matter of morality. 'Whenever there is an unequal distribution of power between two people, the relationship becomes a moral one' (Sergiovanni 2001: 13).

Sources of power and authority

In schools, power derives from a contractual relationship that can impose consequences on those who do not comply. If you don't do what the boss has instructed you to do, he or she can discipline you or make life difficult for you.

Authority can be derived from positive sources:

- **Explanation** – the leader's ability to present a clear and persuasive case for a particular way of thinking. This requires a degree of clarity and respect for the listener.

- **Loyalty** – the leader's appeal that you help out by following a particular course of action, coupled by the shared will to do what is best for the leader and/or the school. This can only happen in a climate of mutual respect and commitment.

- **Track record** – the leader's appeal to experience of how things have worked elsewhere and the suggestion this can be applied to the current situation. To exercise that you need a track record from which to work – either based on personal or researched experience.

Who is in control?

Wouldn't it be a fluffy world if everyone agreed with me!

However, while the desire is to exercise authority, there is a continuum at work here at the extreme ends of which are the control I take as a leader by virtue of my office and the degree to which my team are in shared control of things. This has been diagrammatically represented by Law and Glover (following the continuum of leadership styles devised by Tannenbaum and Schmidt) leading to the diagram shown in Figure 3.1. At the left-hand side the leader has the big degree of control and the team is limited. At the right-hand extreme the team have the big vertical axis and the leader has relinquished control retreating to that little bit at the top. The notes along the bottom provide insights into the sort of management that is taking place at each stage of the continuum. Along the continuum there is a balance between the manager's authority and the freedom of the group. Neither ever totally dominates to gain 100% control – even when you are behaving like a dictator you can't change the way people think and feel (it's true – try it some day!).

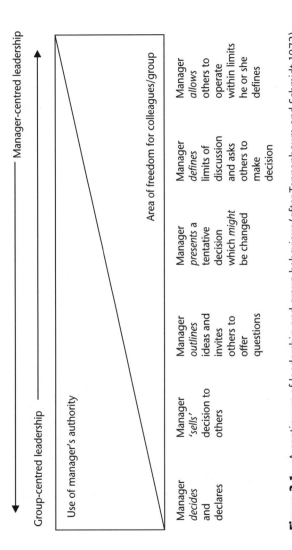

Figure 3.1 A continuum of leadership and group behaviour (after Tannenbaum and Schmidt 1973)

Activity

Map on to the Tannenbaum and Schmidt continuum various instances when you have needed to give a clear, and maybe unpopular, direction and times when things have been more democratic. Have the situations matched the style you have adopted? Are there more instances at one point on the scale than another?

Authoritative leadership

There is no instant fix or strategy for 'instant authority', but applying the thinking behind the ideal suggests some pointers for this sort of leadership:

■ communicate a lot of stuff to a lot of staff. Explain the budget to those who don't manage it, explore dilemmas you face with those who may give a different point of view – talk to staff about the school

■ delegate effectively, involving staff fully in the school see page 30

■ acknowledge when you are saying something contentious, creating planned space for staff to come back with responses – so don't give bad news on a Friday when they're off for the weekend. Give it on a Monday and tell them you'll be around the following day at lunchtime for them to air their responses

■ take time to explain your thinking and receive responses from your team. This can involve stretching nearly every major change over to, at the very least, two meetings, giving time after the first to respond to the team

■ be honest about where you are on the control continuum. If you are taking soundings and agreeing a way forward, make that clear, but don't try and force a decision you have already reached

■ present decisions and plans with confidence and decisiveness. If you are challenged on a decision don't go on the defensive. Ask questions, take notes, show interest and promise to come back on these points, then genuinely take stock of your initial thinking

- don't stand your ground or exercise your power too often. Every time you do this you devalue it and create a more coercive feel to your team

- watch your language – if you have a difficult decision or outcome to communicate to staff say it aloud to yourself beforehand (seriously!)

- use Gillen's three-point sentence when 'standing your ground' on a decision or plan of action that is challenged, or will be difficult. The three parts are 'show empathy, communicate how you feel and state what you want' (Gillen 2002: 143). 'I understand it's a cherished institution and a good fundraiser, however I am concerned at the messages we're sending about healthy eating which is why I am changing the tuck shop.' (Gillen also points out 'however' sounds more positive than 'but'.)

Effective delegation

Five thoughts about delegation:

- Delegate with clarity. Be clear what is being delegated, to whom and what the parameters are around this arrangement.

- Decide what level of delegation is in play.

- Table 3.3 shows varying levels of delegation from carte blanche to puppets on strings!

- Time it. Build a timescale into delegation – whether it's 'We'll meet each term to discuss this' or 'Can I have a weekly report on how this is going'.

- Make sure you show gratitude and give praise in front of other colleagues when a delegated task is being well done.

Table 3.3   Delegation (from Brighouse and Woods 1999)

1	Look into the problem. Give me all the facts. I will decide what to do.
2	Let me know the alternatives available with the pros and cons of each. I will decide which to select.
3	Let me know the criteria for your recommendation, which alternatives you have identified, and which one appears best to you with any risks identified. I will make the decision.
4	Recommend a course of action for my approval.
5	Let me know what you intend to do. Delay action until I approve.
6	Let me know what you intend to do. Do it unless I say not to.
7	Take action. Let me know what you did. Let me know how it turns out.
8	Take action. Communicate with me only if your action is unsuccessful.
9	Take action. No further communication with me is necessary.

Different times, different styles

One point on which various writers on leadership are all agreed are that there will be different situations and phases in the task of leadership that will call for the adoption of different leadership styles.

Sergiovanni (1987) presents the four stages of leadership.

Table 3.4   Stages of leadership

- Bartering – pushing a change; initiating.
- Building – creating the supportive climate during a time of uncertainty.
- Bonding – making a breakthrough and inspiring staff, with common cause.
- Banking – monitoring change as it becomes part of the institution.

He suggests these may be 'thought of as developmental stages each suited to different levels of school competence and excellence' (Sergiovanni 1987: 123). 'Leading by bartering, for example, makes most sense in schools that are not working very well. Leadership by bonding, by contrast, makes sense when basic competence is not the issue and when a healthy interpersonal climate has been established' (Sergiovanni 1987: 124).

I would extend his discussion to suggest that the four stages can apply to any change that the school undertakes, major or minor. A change such as the remodelling of the workforce or changing of job descriptions will follow some or all of these stages, depending on how well it fits with current practice.

Initiation, development and withdrawal

Brighouse and Woods (1999) suggest there are three phases to a headship, somewhat akin to the adoption of different styles. These can be applied to most leadership roles.

Brighouse and Woods issue two warnings for that initiation phase. They counsel against constantly referring to how well things were done in a previous job – a difficult one to follow when that's the one experience you have to draw on, but a tactful point worth bearing in mind. They also warn against those who end up 'measuring the school's progress from the moment they themselves arrived there', noting that 'the really successful leader finds something of value to honour in the legacy they have inherited' (Brighouse and Woods 1999: 68–69).

The second stage is often 'capable of being lengthened by successive waves of renewal' (p.72). They also present a point, three or four years into the development stage, when 'big decisions not grasped in the first phase can be tackled' (p.72), noting that these are often personnel issues.

One of the most valuable features of their analysis is the urging upon us of some realism about that third stage. Thinking through when it could be and having some thoughts about whether we are entering it can be healthy, not just for a leader, but for a school.

Table 3.5 Phases of headship (Brighouse and Woods)

- Initiation – the period of finding out, sometimes involving keeping one's own counsel about things encountered.
- Development – a time of implementing an agenda, with a shift in time as initiatives set in motion continue and tasks that needed day-to-day attention can be come more staggered.
- Decline and withdrawal – the period of moving on either to retirement or a new job.

Step 4

Coaching

Someone once said that 25 years spent in teaching can often be the same year repeated 25 times over. One of the most important and rewarding tasks of leadership is coaching, the progressive development of the staff team. The term coach comes from the old European town of Koks, where horse-drawn carriages were made. Makes me wonder if in my role as coach, I'm meant to be the horse or the cart – but the image carries something of a definition of this task. As coach, we move people.

However, keeping the horse image, coaching is not about driving others or even about telling them where and how to drive. The challenge of effective coaching is to enable others to travel. Through working with staff we enable them to decide on, and travel towards, chosen destinations. It's vital that their hands keep the grip on the reins.

Rather than telling people what to do, the coach enables their independent understanding of what to do, so that people gain ownership of their professional development.

There are similarities to the sporting context. For example, just as Sven-Göran Eriksson wasn't a particularly outstanding footballer but a great coach, so I can easily list teachers I've coached through their professional progress who were way better than me at classroom practice, and yet there I am, coaching away! That's because coaching isn't teaching. Coaching is a different skill. It's about enabling people to do even better.

Keeping in the coaching vein, one vital aspect of coaching is described by the tennis coach, Tim Galleway, when he draws up the following equation (quoted in Parsloe 1995: 27): 'POTENTIAL minus INTERFERENCE equals PERFORMANCE'.

Our job is to highlight the potential and also, crucially, to support colleagues in removing the interference.

At this point it's probably opportune to distinguish the coaching process from performance management. While coaching may form a part of the official function of performance management, the latter is a separate area, linked to progression up the pay spine. Good PM will involve coaching, but good coaching is about developing individuals and appeals to the basic motive within people, namely that they seek personal growth.

■ A spiral process

Spirals are a natural marvel. The plain old snail carves a beautiful, lined shell – each line was once a growing edge, soft and vulnerable. By spiralling, the shell maintains growth through a cycle. The coaching process is a spiral involving the stages of the process in a cycle that returns to its origin – but with growth beyond the starting point. Just as nature uses the spiral for a whole range of growth processes, so the pattern fits this natural professional progress – it's a cycle that grows rather than continually goes round in circles.

Groundwork: relationships

Fostering positive and honest relationships within the staff team is not a part of the coaching process. It's not just something that precedes it or follows after its completion. Good relationships create the context in which coaching can take place. Lose that and the process becomes formal and turgid.

Kate Hopkinson points out that this essential building of rapport is not a technique. 'The essence of real rapport is "authenticity" . . . being present for – and open to – another person in a way that no technique (however skilfully wielded) will facilitate' (Hopkinson in Megginson and Clutterbuck 2005: 30).

That openness and authenticity comes from getting to know our staff – their names, background, home life and family. Chatting about family, holidays, important events in their lives, their background, their enthusiasms – I'm nosey, so want to know everything, but aside from that these are all ways of cultivating relationships with members of staff. It involves tapping into the areas of life that matter most to them – the singing group they organise, the son starting his apprenticeship, the DIY project planned for the summer holidays.

The vital tip here is to remember we're not talking about a 20-minute interview once a year. The building of relationships takes time, throughout the year.

Within the sort of relationship that fosters good coaching there are two complementary aspects at work. Relationships have high and low levels of rapport as well as high and low levels of clarity. Clutterbuck and Ragins (in Megginson and Clutterbuck 2005: 18) map these onto a diagram (see Figure 4.1) that charts the various types of professional dialogue that will take place in different contexts – so in the low rapport/high clarity quadrant the coach and coachee will have tetchy exchanges and argue about the target-setting process. High rapport and low clarity is chummy but ineffective. The ideal is that quadrant that balances a high rapport with a high level of clarity.

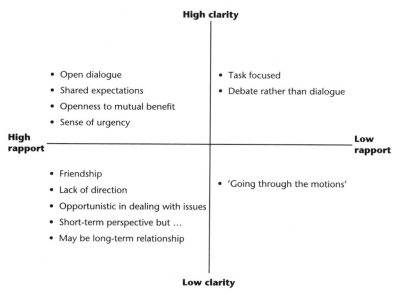

Figure 4.1 Relationship between goal clarity and rapport in mentoring (Reproduced with permission from *Mentoring and Diversity*, by Clutterbuck and Ragins.)

Activity

How well do I know the team?

Make a list of the staff in your school and try to think of one or two things you know about each of them that would provide the starting point for a conversation – the avid reader, the one whose son recently graduated. What sorts of things do you know?

Groundwork: acknowledge the staff

So we need to build rapport. As we discover the things that fire up individuals and explore their expertise and enthusiasm in various aspects of the curriculum, we cultivate a relationship that moves beyond rapport with a sense of purpose.

This involves acknowledging the contribution staff make to the whole school. Acknowledge people's comments, contributions and ideas – preferably in front of others so you make your acknowledgement public. Write notes or cards of thanks. The main thing here is to make sure this doesn't sink to some formal exercise in patronising staff. General and bland 'Thanks' doesn't work. Rather than 'Thanks for doing a great job' we're the ones saying 'It's been a tough week in this class but you've kept them on task, particularly that gaggle of lads that are always falling out. Thanks for that'. Make the 'thank-yous' specific.

Groundwork: overview

As a school leader, the coaching of staff fits into the other aspects of a vision for the school. The reorganising of classes into year teams may offer roles for potential leaders. The development of new initiatives or involvement in LEA projects may provide space for personnel to develop. Parsloe uses the image of the successful team coach being like the heli-copter, rising above day-to-day events and taking an overview of what is happening. The control and height enables us to take a tactical and strategic view, and Parsloe contrasts it with the 'seagull' coach who 'flies in, circles around, makes a lot of noise, swoops down and craps on a few people before quickly flying off again' (Parsloe 1995: 29).

■ Coaching: the process

Having created the right conditions for coaching, the process itself
follows the spiral described earlier.

Process: review

The first step in the process involves setting aside time to talk with staff
about how things are going, both in the long-term career frame and in
the more specific past year or two in the current job. When doing this
it's important to keep trying to home in on specific examples of real
situations, so if a member of staff brings 'I feel discipline is going down
the tubes' to the conversation we need to ask specifics, such as which
children are involved and for examples of when this has happened.

Megginson and Clutterbuck (2005) provide a useful model for
clarifying situations, suggesting we need to step in and out of the
individual's perspective and explore the rational and emotional aspects
of this experience.

Stepping in involves taking on the perspective of the coachee and
working with them so that we gain an understanding of what they are
thinking and feeling. This can be a rational unpicking of a situation or
an emotional empathising with how it feels.

Stepping out involves a distancing from the situation where we use
our distance to enable others to see the situation from the outside –
from our point of view or that of another 'outsider'.

We need to step in and out, throughout the coaching process.

Questions

Questioning is a key ingredient of the coaching process. It's the way we
keep people's hands on the reins and find the difference between
guiding and telling. When we ask questions we enable coachees to find
their own way to their own answers – answers they will then own more
fully than those that are imposed into the conversation.

As a means of remembering the importance of questioning, as
opposed to 'telling', Parsloe provides the guideline that coaching should
be split into '80 per cent asking questions and only 20 per cent giving
answers' (Parsloe 1995: 75).

However, I would just balance this up with the note of caution. In entering into professional discussions I'm sure coachees don't expect the Spanish Inquisition (no one expects them!). There is a danger that the constant barrage of questioning can prove as forced and off-putting as directed telling. Keep asking yourself if the questioning is intrusive or causing a coachee to go on the defensive – because this will reduce the relationship to a formal business.

To be effective questioning must:

- combine open questions that explore around a subject ('Tell me more about what the children do in investigative maths?') with the sorts of questions that narrow down to specifics ('Why do you think that group always presents you with a problem?');

- allow spaces for reflection on the current point. Pressing on with a barrage of questions can mean that none of them are answered thoroughly. Allowing some space for silence can provide space for a further elaboration on an answer;

- genuinely involve the questioner. Remember we're not grilling a defendant, we're working with a colleague. Phrases like 'That's interesting' and 'I wonder why that happens' keep the discussion going and are a green light to the coachee to think and say more – they also keep us in the discussion rather than in the role of distanced observers;

- allow for answers. The golden rule is: give people time to answer. Few things are more hateful than someone asking a question and then butting in before an answer is finished. Reflect on the answers, ask for clarification, and genuinely listen to them and allow them to build the conversation.

Bear in mind there is a time for telling as well as asking. Landsberg suggests this will be when the coach has genuine expertise to offer or when there is a critical point of direction to be given, 'where failure would lead to disaster' (Landsberg 1996: 9).

Five questions

A quick list – five question structures I keep in mind for coaching discussions. They work on the assumption the coachee is moving from x to y. You need to trim them to fill in x and y, but they pick apart the main things we need to consider in coaching discussions.

- what would y look like
- why do we need to change x?
- what would you do in the short/medium/long term to make y?
- what are the main blockages that could stop this move from x to y?
- how will you know y is being reached?

Timing

Effective coaching is well timed.

Parsloe gives the guideline that coaching sessions should be between 30 and 75 minutes (Parsloe 1995: 72). Within such sessions I would suggest there needs to be a pause every 10 to 15 minutes to recap on where the discussion has got to thus far.

It's also important to note that, while the formal sessions may be of that length, there is also important work that takes place in the snatched 5-minute discussions that follow the more formal sessions. The new initiative needs a brief 'How did it go?' at its conclusion.

Listening skills

I once did half a counselling course. I couldn't cope with day two. All that stuff about leaning forward and cocking your head to one side was causing me stress. However, there are distinct skills to be developed that can make us better listeners. Countless articles and books list what good listeners do, but the following qualities stand out for me. Good listeners:

- have body language that demonstrates engagement – leaning slightly forward, indicating engagement in the conversation, rather than slouching away in boredom. However, you don't have to cock your head!

- give space for answers without interrupting or jumping in with advice;

- put questions to the statements, teasing out some specific details;

- maintain a good level of eye contact – though avoid the bug-eyed staring contest that some people bring back from 'listening skills' courses. This habit can prove too much like meeting with a chameleon;

- use gestures and short 'right', 'mmm' and 'I remember' types of responses to communicate continued engagement;

- focus on the conversation. Benton offers the advice that we need to 'silence all internal dialogue' (Benton 1994: 81). Yes, I know that sounds like a Jedi proverb but it is still important to banish thoughts about other things from our minds.

Process: goals

If I had to pick out one part of this process as the important one, the one worth devoting time and energy to making sure we've got it just right – this is it. 'Time spent on gaining clarity and commitment at this stage will be repaid many times over' (Megginson and Clutterbuck 2005: 37).

Goals need to provide a positive stimulus to the coachee. Researchers tell us that people have a positive and negative emotional attractor (PEA and NEA). The PEA is evoked when people develop their image of their ideal self, when they dream and hope. The NEA is aroused by a focus on weakness and what we do wrong. 'The PEA allows you to open yourself to new possibilities. The NEA pushes you to fix things that are wrong. The PEA pulls us forward, whereas the NEA inhibits progress and turns us off.'

To quote one illuminating insight into how the NEA operates: 'Have you ever wondered why it is so hard for most people to lose weight? We believe it's because this is a negatively conceived goal.'

The sum of these insights is simple: 'To make a sustainable change in habits or behaviour, a person needs to start with the PEA and move through the NEA' (Boyzatis, Howard, Kapisara and Taylor 2004: 29).

If a teacher fails to sustain good discipline they need to be given a goal through tapping their own hopes for how orderly and calm their classroom can be – the negative failure to discipline will be tackled by that positive move forward. If a teaching assistant is ill prepared the goal needs to grow from the positive image of what they do and how they can support the group they work with. Beginning with the negative just pushes people into a defensive, clammed up mode.

Goals should spring from a coachee's idea of the desired outcome of their personal development and part of the coach's task is to support the ascertaining of that vision.

It would be hard to provide an exhaustive list of goals, but in a school context possibilities include:

- **classroom practice and performance goals –**

  - improving an aspect of classroom practice

  - improving the performance of a particular group of children;

- **professional development goals –**

  - taking on a specific responsibility

  - developing a particular aspect of curricular responsibility

  - taking on a leadership role within the staff team;

- **personal knowledge, skills and understanding goals –**

  - engaging in a piece of research and disseminating findings

  - gaining and using knowledge of a new area of practice.

A big difference enters this process if the goals being set are in some way connected to some wider development, such as the whole-school improvement plan or some local authority initiative. Such linkage can both secure a goal, resource it and keep us all on our toes to follow it through.

Deciding goals
There are a few tactics we can deploy when it comes to drawing goals out of colleagues. These include:

Future speech
In his work on goals, Stephen Covey (1989) suggests we morbidly imagine the oration at our own funeral. There is something to be said

for imagining what someone would say about success in a few years time. It helps to ask staff what reaching a goal would look like – 'If I saw this goal accomplished what sorts of things would I see?' It's about visualising success then picking apart the component elements.

Big to small, small to big

Start with small details and work to a bigger picture or vice versa. Some staff will be very general 'I'd like to improve everything', others too specific – 'I can't stop Lorraine and Joanne talking to each other'. Starting at either point work in the opposite direction – so the 'everything' needs to be challenged with an 'OK, let's list everything – what's at the top of the list'. Whereas Lorraine and Joanne need to be grown into a more reasonable goal – 'Are they the only ones?', 'What's it telling us about the classroom environment?', 'Which bit of the discipline policy would we develop to sort that out?'

Extremes

In this technique, suggested by Megginson and Clutterbuck (2005: 46) it's suggested that we name the extremes from which we want to change and to which we wish to change. We assign emotive labels to these – so in the case of a colleague who had an issue with keeping the classroom tidy the two extremes could be called 'Pristine and ordered' and 'Shit tip'. These are the extremes on the spectrum to which questions can be put such as:

- where are you on the spectrum in between?
- where do you want to be?
- what would the consequences be of moving?

In my experience, just having the idea of naming the two extremes provides a useful framework that seems to 'hem in' the discussion.

Activity

Think through some of the goals staff already have set. How could the sort of discussion outlined here enhance the setting or revising of goals?

Process: engagement

Many models of coaching move from goals to action but I would suggest there is a stage in between, at which the coachee becomes engaged in the goal. It is adapted from a stage Cambourne highlights in the learning processes children undertake (Cambourne 1995: 52). I see it as involving the coachee in being clear about three things and therefore taking on ownership both of the goals and change process. The conviction needs to be there that:

a. the goals can be achieved

b. they are worth achieving

c. it is safe to risk having a go – the consequences of any failure will not be dire.

The other vital component of engagement is something to do immediately. Goals that are to be tackled in the future risk being neglected and forgotten. Goal setting needs to lead to an action stage that, for the sake of solid engagement, has an immediate action of some sort.

Process: action stage

The coaching process needs a clearly identified set of actions planned into a set period of time – whether this is a month, term or year. This is not the place to look at formats for action planning or suggest actions that can match some of the goals that could be set. From the point of view of good coaching practice the action stage should include the following:

Creativity
Don't be constrained by the regular actions done by everyone else – be prepared to consider the more creative and less conventional actions.

Workplace learning
Going out on courses is not the answer – and it's costly. Look at what sort of experimental and observational learning and reflection can be had from the day-to-day school setting, whether in the coachee's current class or through visits to the classrooms of other colleagues.

Applied input

Where courses or resourcing are deployed there needs to be a clear focus on the outcome and how these are contributing to reaching the goal.

Review along the way

Build regular opportunities to review goals and actions into the timescale – though not over regular. People need time to work things through, not the hassle of overbearing accountability.

Stay involved

From the outset there needs to be an agreement as to how the coach maintains involvement in the process being coached. Will this be through direct involvement or occasional review?

It's useful to ask staff to give some sort of brief written note feeding back from professional development opportunities, such as courses or visits to other schools. Here again, the focus should be on how the activity has impacted on the goal.

Action ideas

The following actions are useful ones to put into the development process:

- build some form of liaison into the process, such that the coachee has to connect up with others

- specify something that is to be researched, an area where further learning is to be garnered

- seek opportunities or individual goals to be aired in a whole school context – possibly through input in a staff meeting or production of a particular resource.

Realistic resourcing

Watch out for actions that involve high maintenance – 'To use an understanding of teaching methods in Bermuda I will first need . . .' Make sure any supply costs or resource needs are clear and agreed from the outset, so that the coachee can engage with commitment in a process that will happen.

Ask around

Look at what other leaders are putting forward in their schools for their staff. Some examples may turn you cold – but, for me, this has been an invaluable source of ideas.

Process: review and re-set

Like any organic process, growth through actions needs constant input to sustain itself. This needs to be planned at the inception of the process. Don't end the goals and action discussion without getting out the diary and asking 'By when should we pick up on this?' The catching up can take many forms: written memo, quick cuppa and chat, formal meeting, exchange of emails – whatever is going to work best. But plan short – don't riddle the next twelve months with half-hour meetings every month. Too much planned meeting breaks down too easily leaving nothing in its place. Small and manageable is more likely to happen.

As people grow in their work they need to be shown what sort of positive changes they are making. Taffinder suggests that one essential workplace reward is the simple experience of being told how we fit in and contribute to the organisation as a whole (Taffinder 2000: 146). The message that their success fits into your vision also reinforces your leadership of the team.

Process: celebrate

When people do things for our school we celebrate their actions. Nothing is more sick-bucketing than the hero head who 'Turned the school around' displaying, with every stripe in their suit and pad in their shoulder, the image of the lone individual who did it all without any help from the lazy sods in the staff room. As if! When leaders steal the glory for their actions they demoralise the rest of the team.

Far better to pepper letters home, mentions in staff meeting and other gatherings and references in the governors report with the names of others. Jowett, the great nineteenth-century Greek scholar and educator once wisely suggested 'The way to get things done is not to mind who gets the credit of doing them' (quoted in Phillips 1993: 6).

■ Blockages

As expected, a chapter on this lovely and organic process ends with a section on its problems. Well you didn't think life was that fluffy, did you? Here is a list of six common blockages to achieving the goals of coaching with some thoughts about how they can be handled.

1 Weak systems
If the system for setting goals and following through with action isn't clear, other short-term priorities will swamp the longer-term process of staff development.

2 Initial reluctance
Staff can be initially reluctant to enter into this sort of process, particularly if experiences elsewhere have conditioned them to think negatively about the process. In such cases time needs to be taken building a relationship and clearly outlining a personal vision of how coaching should work both for the staff as well as the school.

3 Worms fit for only for the mud
AKA . . . those who are not fit to be on the planet, the self-professed failures who declare that they are just not good enough to do anything and who couldn't possibly set a goal because they are such detritus. Caricature aside, the main issue in goal setting is often not about tackling incapabilities. It's about getting them to believe in their capabilities. Make sure the review process brings in clear and specifically identified examples of the positive contribution a colleague makes to the school, such that coaching will just provide a natural extension to this current picture.

4 Can do, will do
Staff will demonstrate varying levels of willingness and ability. Heller and Hindle identify four character types (1998: 376):

■ can do-will do: happy to take responsibility and able to carry out resultant tasks effectively

■ can do-won't do: has the ability but, for whatever reason, won't take the responsibility

■ will do-can't do: eager enough but just not able to carry out the tasks necessary

■ can't do-won't do: lacks motivation and ability.

Depending on what you are faced with you need to apply an appropriate level of direction and support.

■ can do-will do – these need space to get on with the job but be sure to offer support, direction and praise as they steam onwards;

■ can do-won't do – here there is a need for clear direction and expectation, then close watching in case they play silly buggers. Can they be brought to see the value of their contribution?

■ will do-can't do – acknowledge and welcome the enthusiasm, provide the support they need to access the job they want to do and keep your patience;

■ can't do-won't do – here the relationship will become very formal and may lead to proceedings. It's important to know when you are encountering this type – offer the support and give clear direction, being realistic about what you can achieve, then call in your adviser or whoever else is needed to help you see the way ahead on this one. Difficult stuff!

5 Specifics

Vagueness is the plughole that sucks performance. From the earliest stage we need to be on the lookout for specific hitches in a planned set of coached actions. It's no good planning to work with a colleague on their teaching of mental maths if the timetable arrangement means they never teach the subject. List the specifics early and diary in the time when they need to be tackled.

6 Red herrings

Parsloe raises this as a real problem in some professional discussion (Parsloe 1995: 73). We need to be mindful of their existence and keep the conversation coming back to the subject under discussion. He recommends that action points are written down, keeping the focus.

■ Six final points about coaching

1 It requires a degree of self-awareness. We need to know when we're slipping from asking to telling. We need to know the areas where we ourselves need to make personal progress. We need to gauge our relationships with those we coach.

2 It requires modelling. I can recall working for a head teacher who, when the school was suddenly faced with amalgamation, said in a conversation 'It's a pain – but, actually, I quite thrive on change'. She presented a role model and a different way of looking at the situation . . . and proved to be an excellent coach.

3 It thrives in a climate of stimulation and ideas. It thrives in a climate where we are cutting articles out of the education press and passing them around, where our discussion can be steered towards a thoughtfulness about the job we do.

4 It can dry up if we get too analytical. These are professional discussions – not the psychiatrist's chair. We need to keep them focused on the job and the improvement of our practice.

5 It can dry up if it becomes too formal. It can end up being a time-serving activity, done so we can say we did it. It thrives where we combine a formal structure with some informal enthusiasm.

6 It trusts people. It gives some space for them to develop in diverse and interesting ways.

Step 5

Leading the team

'Managers devolve, leaders involve' (Leigh and Maynard 1996: 65) – this strikes me as a succinct distinction between leadership and management. As leaders one of our key roles is that of engaging with others in a team. The authors of this definition quote the example of Dyson vacuum cleaners, where everyone who begins to work for the company makes a vacuum cleaner on the first day. In doing so they are all getting involved in the core business of the company. It's something shared.

At every level of the primary school we find ourselves involved in the workings of teams. We have a governing body, it has its sub-committees, there is a whole staff team, they occasionally break into smaller working groups, our supervisory staff will be brought together, a group of parents will work together on a Summer Fayre. Everywhere you look people are working together.

This picture raises the question – what is it that makes a group of people into a team? Groups can be together for a whole host of reasons, but what makes them a team?

Think of a game of charades at a party. The partygoers are divided into smaller groups and engage in a competitive game, with the aim of winning. The crowd of partygoers has now become two distinct teams, aiming to win. 'When a group of people have a goal, in this case to have a great time and win at charades, you create teams' (Owen, Hodgson and Gazzard 2004: 345).

▨ The distinction matters

I can recall working in a school where everyone did their own thing. There was the occasional staff meeting, but nothing regular, and the ones called were more briefings. There was no common purpose – and consequently I wouldn't describe that group of staff as a team.

When a complex task is approached by a group working on it together you have a team. If the task is mundane they don't necessarily need to engage with each other. If the need for co-operation is low they won't connect either. When the two come together we need a team (Casey 1993: 37). The conjunction of complexity and co-operation is the point at which we need to work as a team.

One other important distinction should be made between the formal and the informal element of teams. Some are formally designated to, for example, construct a budget for the school. That's great – but I would also place great store by the group of four staff who chat one lunchtime about an idea, organise who will do what and end up organising some fantastic project or school trip. Here again, the defining feature was the purpose.

▨ 'What?' and 'How?': the components of teamwork

The two vital components of a team are the 'What?', as in 'What's wanted of us?', 'What is our purpose?' and the 'How', as in 'How do we achieve this?', 'How do we proceed?'

These two questions form the following list of needs any team will face:

- ■ clear objectives
- ■ team ethos
- ■ interpersonal effectiveness
- ■ varied roles
- ■ team development
- ■ time

- a process for decision making
- good communication.

Clear objectives

A team needs to know what it is being asked to do and the clearer the goal the more effective the team will be. So a staff team at the start of a meeting needs a clear idea of what it's expected to achieve over the course of its meeting, whereas a drifting agenda will result in the team fragmenting and becoming less co-operative.

Part of working effectively as a team leader or member is to occasionally remind everyone of their core purpose. Once the school has its mission statement and set of aims, one of the jobs of leadership is to constantly make the link between these and the various initiatives on which the school embarks, slipping the core purpose of the school into the discussion.

A team can know its purpose. It also needs clear indication of how much slack it has to pursue that purpose.

To this end leadership involves clarifying the purpose of a team and its level of responsibility.

What is it there for?

- consultation – just presenting views
- devising – devising a range of options
- decision – having the authority to finalise the way forward
- planning – implementing a decision already taken
- reviewing – analysing something with a view towards evaluation and suggested changes.

To take blunt examples, can it direct other staff? can it take over staff development time? can it spend any money? Whether it's the small group organising the residential or whole staff reappraisal of the teaching of history, the team needs to know what it can and can't do. You might want to look back at the section on delegation on page 30 and the can do-will do idea on page 46. When you delegate to a team you need to know exactly what shape they are in to handle the delegation. If you have three 'can't do' types with one 'can do', it could end up with conflict or one person being overburdened. Although delegation involves taking a step away these are the sorts of team features worth watching out for.

Ultimately, though, delegation is about trusting teams to get on with the task. I like Warren Bennis's inspiring notion that: 'The leader is able to realise his or her dream only if the others are free to do exceptional work' (quoted in Birkinshaw and Crainer 2002: 103).

Clear objectives, including the parameters of a task, are the 'What?' of teamwork. The following facts tackle the 'How?'

Team ethos

Every team, staff team, governing body, parents group – they all have a distinct culture. Handy identifies these in diagrammatic form, suggesting that they have an application to education (Handy 1976: 180ff; Handy and Aitken 1986: 85ff).

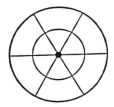

The club culture is symbolised by a web. There's a pivotal inner point and close-knit inner circle with an outer group. Handy suggests the business example would be the family firm, though I've encountered some smaller schools that operate like this.

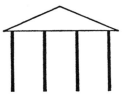

The role culture is symbolised by the temple. In this culture your job title matters a bit more than your interpersonal connection. It's a more bureaucratic form, the advantage being the stability it can offer.

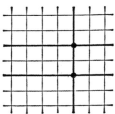

The task culture is a net. Here the emphasis is on problem solving. People group and regroup to tackle specific tasks. Your knowledge can matter more than your role, but it can be difficult to keep control of what's going on.

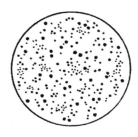 The person culture consists of individuals. There are few controls and individuals operate as dots within the circle. Handy notes that, while few organisations could actually operate like this, it can be the case that certain individuals have this mindset, making them difficult to manage.

Like any organisation, a school will have a mix of cultures, but there will be dominant forces at work. Effective teamwork requires an idea of what culture predominates and importing of aspects that are useful from the others. For example, if control is too tight, maybe individuals need a bit of autonomy. If roles are stifling effective work, maybe there's a need for a focus on the tasks in hand. If individualism has created a laissez faire culture, maybe it's time the roles were reviewed.

One cautionary note worth heeding can be found in Gibson and Zellmer-Bruhn's (2001) work on metaphors of teams. They look at some of the metaphors used to describe teams, such as images of family or an army going to battle. They urge us to watch out for the way leaders can have different images in mind to the ones borne by the rest of the team. So the school leader who talks of 'the battle ahead', 'going over the top' and 'attacking' isn't one I would feel at ease with. I would be much happier with images of playing football or making cake! 'If some of the team members picture their team as doing battle . . . while others view the time as a loosely connected open community, conflict . . . is likely to ensue' (Gibson and Zellmer-Buhn 2001: 300).

Leading the culture

Leadership involves the cultivation of the right ethos for the right situation. The main ways of doing this will be the language we use and the example we set. Two quick notes on this. Our team ethos is spread by the pronouns we use. Leaders grate when they constantly say 'I . . . I . . .' – what are they wanting? Worship? Listen to an inspiring leader, a Mandela or a Churchill, and you hear 'we' and 'us' language, involving all. Secondly our examples promote the ethos. A story is told of a woman who brought her son to Gandhi with the complaint that he had rotten teeth. Gandhi told her to come back in a week's time and he would answer her problem.

A week later she returned and Gandhi offered the simple answer 'Have him eat less sugar'. The woman asked 'Why couldn't you tell me that last week?'. 'Because last week' the great leader replied 'I was still eating sugar'. If we say 'every child matters' we'll make the time for the children in our own school. If we believe deadlines matter, we will keep them. We will set the example (Owen, Hodgson and Gazzard 2004: 201).

Established teams

In many cases leaders in education are not drawing together a new team, they are stepping into an established one. In these situations it's vital to take time to look at the culture. The other significant piece of sensitivity to the situation is to look at how individuals fit into the culture. If it's a chummy little circle is there an isolated dot who isn't a part of it? Is there a little team of effective task workers struggling to get things done in a role-dominated structure?

Interpersonal effectiveness

The single most important process factor in any team is the fact that it is made up of people, working as a whole but each bringing their own personalities. Rapport, the glue that can hold them together, is worth investing effort in.

Rapport

There needs to be a rapport between a team. We also need to avoid the notion that effective teams love each other and share their packed lunches. Friendship can be a good bond (it can also be an obstruction) but rapport is about a good team relationship. What we're looking for is:

- **awareness:** teams need to be confident in each other. This sometimes means being realistic about each other's strengths and failings

- **respect:** there needs to be an awareness of what each individual brings to the team

- **commitment:** 'teams are the basis for individual success' (Scase in Birkinshaw and Crainer 2002: 93). Teams work when individuals know they cannot get the job done without the others. There needs to be a commitment to work together.

Bottom line in all this – there is a chemistry and if we could bottle it we would make a million. There are activities and exercises we can do under the heading of team building (see 'Team building' box below), but that vital ingredient of rapport is elusive, precious and worth working at.

Team building

What we're wanting is for them to know each other, respect each other and commit to each other. Team building is about taking time to foster these relationships.

- Warm up working times with competitive tasks for your teams. These can be straightforward games, such as a set of Dingbats or trivia questions with the challenge for each team to complete as many as they can.

- When it comes to building and renewing links between people, a list of 'Find someone who' tasks provides a good ice breaker (e.g. 'Find someone who can ride a horse', 'Find someone who has seen all the Star Wars films'). This works well if you can slip in some facts about your staff that are both alluring and not widely known, e.g. 'Find someone who has had a meal with Mick Jagger'.

- Give teams tasks that involve listening to each other talk about more than the simple task. Instead of going straight for the drawing up of a geography policy, ask a team to spend five minutes recalling their own experience of travel, or their own recollections of geography teaching at school.

- Spread things. Find out interesting facts about staff and make sure they are drawn into conversation either informally or brought up as examples in staff development. The fact a member of a team worked in a 70s 'free school' is worth knowing and drawing on – it's an experience with learning to offer.

- Organise times together – or better still have a fantastic 'social secretary' on your staff. Whether it's the glass of red wine at the end of Friday, a meal out, or a trip to the theatre, these are not just frills, these are vital parts of the team building task.

Varied roles

Watch any team at work – someone will be leading, someone will be coming up with ideas, someone will be annoying the pants off all the others. There are certain roles that emerge, analysed in some detail by various writers (e.g. Belbin 1993). The table that follows isn't anywhere like as scientific but gives a list of some roles that come to the fore, again and again.

Table 5.1 Varied roles

Role	Key features of this team member	How a leader cultivates such a member
Leader	■ when everyone is sitting down, will pick up the agenda and say 'Right, let's get on with it' ■ is prepared to give or suggest direction to others	■ recognise the budding or competent leader, an asset to your school ■ cultivate the qualities that give leadership ■ watch that this person isn't irritating others, if so it could be worth just mentioning how valued their lead is but how diplomatic they need to be
Critic	■ finds the problem in what is suggested ■ can see why something wouldn't work and has a long memory of things that haven't worked in the past	■ recognise the positive contribution made ■ note criticisms but turn to the critic for positive input ('It's a good job you identified that problem – so how would you tackle it?') ■ use the fact someone else has suggested something as a way of slapping them down – 'I wouldn't want to dismiss what Jenny has just said', is a way of saying 'Hold off a mo'

(continued)

Ideas factory	■ comes up with new thinking ■ suggests ideas that are completely stupid	■ recognise the person who will be more creative than you ■ accept and listen to ideas ■ raise questions in a way that smiles – in a way that shows you are glad for the suggestion but . . .
Potato	■ is there because someone sent them ■ won't contribute and doesn't want to act on the basis of others' contribution	■ recognise the need for a metaphorical kick up the pants ■ try tagging their contribution to another more active member's ('Could you and Jo work on that aspect of the plan?') ■ if needs be take them to one side and discuss the matter but – see below – start from the positive ■ if all else fails, grin and bear them
Bag of nerves	■ doesn't feel confident to contribute but wants to get the job done	■ recognise someone whose contribution hasn't come out (why are these people so often support staff?) ■ ask them directly or in the run up to a meeting for an opinion. Saying 'Tell them what you were saying to me the other day' can open this person up ■ watch out for the meeting squeezing them out. Occasionally, just saying 'Cassie, what do you think?' may just get a nod of the head – but it at times it will get a fuller contribution

(*continued*)

Vagary	■ (bit like ideas but) talks in hazy terms no-one can really grasp	■ recognise contributions – but your job is to sharpen them ■ ask precise questions ■ tie down ideas to specific times and places ■ ask for 'short answers'
Precision instrument	■ ties matters down to specifics ■ won't let vagaries go by unchallenged	■ recognise the net through which mistakes won't easily slip ■ ask them to take the minutes! ■ identify the positives in this contribution ■ be the one who occasionally says 'OK, let's get down to detail later – before that, let's explore the ideas some more'

Activity

Think through a current or previous staff team. How do they match up to the characters outlined in the team roles box (see Table 5.1)? Does this give an indication as to how certain people should be managed?

Team development

Teams are organic things – that term always makes me think of mould or yoghurt – but this means teams grow and develop and there are some specific features of that we need to be aware of.

Growth and cultivation

The way a team works will alter over time. Four stages are commonly perceived in the life of any team (Tuckman 1965).

1　Forming – the team get together and start working as a team.

2　Storming – conflicts arise as we realise where we are going to differ and start differing.

3 Norming – norms of working relationships are asserted.

4 Performing – the team works productively and 'group energy is channelled into the task' (Tuckman 1965: 396).

In each of these stages the leader who either leads a team, supports it or participates can meet certain needs.

■ Overarching all is the need to know when a stage is part of the normal development of the team – storming isn't breakdown, its maturation.

■ Identify the phase for the team both as a phase with its own identity and as part of fuller process, giving the optimistic picture of where such a process can lead.

■ Through using a different model of development, one of the jobs of a leader is to help the group move through these stages of development. This can't be rushed but the various stages can be identified.

Difficulties

Find me a team that works without difficulties (apart from 'The Osmonds').

In some ways you need them – how else do you refine ideas and experience creativity if there's no push and shove in the process.

The difficult traits people exhibit include:

■ obstruction 'This won't work – nothing ever works'

■ disconnection 'Do whatever you want – am I bothered?'

■ laggardism 'We've always done it this way'

■ know-it-all 'yeah, yeah, I know, I know'

■ corpses '. . .' (they just sit there saying sod all).

There are various ways of dealing with difficult characters – and most depend on the difficulty. A book like *Managing People* (in this series) will help in this area, but the 'you; them; others' thinking below provides some general ways of creating more positive relationships with the people you'd ideally like to shoot.

To begin with we need to have good, positive thinking about people. No-one can teach another person an attitude but, for the record, here's a standpoint I adopt.

These people aren't behaving like this because they are bad. They have reasons – maybe deep motives – for doing even the most annoying things. Ultimately I want to win them over. I want to work with them.

The rest comes down to how **you, they** and **others** relate.

You:

- Keep cool. You will gain nothing by shouting, getting stroppy or finding ways to needle them. Keep the moral high ground.

- Think – am I to learn something here? Sometimes the critic or the laggard may be telling us things we should listen to.

- Brush away the unhelpfulness. They will get to you! Keep their whinging or their daft comments in perspective. Brush off their comments and complaints. You work on the stuff worth listening to.

They:

- Respect what you can respect. If they have more years of teaching than you – respect the fact. If they think of things you don't – point it out.

- Ally them to your cause – if the change is afoot and someone needs to join you at an LEA briefing on it, take them with you. Give them the special role.

- Ask their opinion. Meet with them, explain your dilemmas, ask what they would do in your shoes.

- Give them informal time. Pop into class at the end of the day on some pretext and chat a while, less formally.

Others:

- Don't gossip about them in the staff room and don't be there while they are being gossiped about.

- Energise the behaviours in others that are at odds with these negative behaviours – the staff who always give that extra 200 per cent when someone is getting away with 50 per cent need to have their extra input acknowledged. Don't do this to bully them, do it to foster the right climate around them.

- Talk to someone – an appropriate colleague in school or an adviser or professional friend outside.

Activity

Analyse tensions we have encountered in the teams we have worked with, looking at how the you/them/others have operated in these difficulties. Have they been largely within the team? Have we been witnesses or directly involved? How have we handled these situations?

Participation

'Trying to force someone's enrolment is like shouting "grow" at a plant' (Leigh and Maynard 1996: 66)

There are people who are semi-detached from the team and need to be brought in, but it is impossible to force this. They will only engage when they see the three components of engagement that motivate our learners as well as our adults, quoted earlier (Cambourne 1998: 52):

> I can do it
> it is worth doing
> there is no threat to me if I fail.

From the leader's point of view, these people need direction as to how their skills match the task and why they are needed. It's about pointing out how their contribution is vital to the success of the wider project. It's about giving safe environments for them to have a go – so if it's their first time leading a group ask them to do it once, rather than for the next twelve weeks.

The wheels of a team are also well oiled by a leader who identifies with some clarity how each member contributes specifically to it. Saying 'If you didn't do this, then . . .' is a vital way of saying 'We need what you do . . . so do us some more'.

It's about satisfying that basic, motivating need of belonging and making a contribution that is valued. It's what you get out of bed for.

An image to use

The image opposite was handed to me by a first-class leadership trainer, Alan Vaughn, as part of some training for my management team in my first headship. It's a graphic presentation of how different people fit together in any situation, produced by an equally inspiring youth work trainer, Pip Wilson. On it I can see myself at different stages in the working week, I can see the people I gravitate to, the ones I avoid. It's a powerful tool for opening discussion on how we are as people and how we work together, the feelings we bring to our work and the way it

Time

Teams need productive time to do the job.

This brings us to the issue of meetings. They are a necessary part of team performance and here are a few useful ingredients.

Icebreaking

Someone needs to break the ice. Faced with a challenge or an issue to pursue some teams may cope with the blank sheet of paper. Others will need some support at the start.

Finding some point that pertains to the matter in hand, they can be asked to jot down some thoughts and share them.

They can be asked to each share a brief statement, such as what they currently know about the topic in hand.

One good rule for a team tackling a task is to try and have everyone speaking within the first ten minutes.

Creativity

It's vital that team members are open to any suggestion and do not stamp down on contributions.

We explored the importance of this sort of wider thinking in our chapter on vision.

Team awareness

It pays to know a staff. For example, in meetings, who will contribute, who won't (unless prompted)? Who will hog the discussion? Blanchard writes of the leader taking the role of a 'participant observer' (Blanchard 2004: 24) in such settings. It is important to have the twin track approach to such meetings – we're there both to tackle whatever is being discussed, solve the problem, propose the resolutions etc. We're also there to make this room of people work well.

Respect

Teams thrive on respect – genuine respect. This is fostered by realising how much we need others in the team. I work on a close-knit estate. I can't engage parents in my school half as well as some of the staff who know them from way back, who have lived in this community. I can't do it without them. That sort of thinking is about respect. It's about remembering Blanchard's wise guideline: 'None of us is smarter than all of us' (Blanchard 2004: 15).

A process for decision making

It's budget setting time. The issue is whether to allocate £14k or £18k to curriculum resources. There's a strong view the £4k difference should be spent on a new whiteboard for the computer suite.

Ultimately a team needs to reach a decision. How do we do that? The aim here should be to ensure consensus is reached – the broad view of the team – rather than unanimous and total approval of any outcomes, and this should be clear in the purpose of the team. Without this, it is possible to end up in a log jam with one team member unhappy at the direction in which things are going. Try to avoid votes – they leave a group clearly turned down and the very act of moving to a vote is a sign that consensus is out of reach

Where there is a difference of opinion it's important to look at how significant is the issue on which the disagreement remains. This is £4k so it's a bigger decision than if it were whether to allocate £400 to First Aid resources. During team work it's important to keep the scale in mind. A good team skill is to know what are the issues that are at the serious end of your scale (as £400 may be to the person responsible for managing first aid).

Poke into the log jam. Why are we here? Why can't I see the need for that whiteboard? Why are you so obsessed with it? Who says we need it and why?

Seek win/win situations. Stephen Covey describes the four outcomes that can result from a disagreement:

- lose/lose – both of us don't get what we
- win/lose – one of us gets what we want and the other is defeated
- win/win – we both get what we want (Covey 1989: 206).

Aim for a situation in which no-one loses and both gain from the discussion: 'Let's divide up the curriculum budget set at 20k and see if we can make savings of up to 4k by asking people to trim back on last year's figures', 'Let's take 2k from the general ICT budget and 2k from the curriculum budget'.

Good communication

The final essential for good teamwork is effective communication. Talk to disgruntled school staff and you will often find the problems they have come down to communication.

Any team needs:

- an agreed way of getting messages out to the whole team – if it's a bulletin board in the staff room, that's it. You can't then expect some vital message via a post-it note on the classroom door not to be missed or lost in the course of the day;

- responsibility shared to make sure messages are received – if we agree to use pigeonholes, check yours. This can be a vital step in ensuring communication works. An agreement that once a day we will all read our emails means we all now know how to get a message to everyone – and we trust it will be read;

■ filters – members of teams only need the stuff they need. We need to be careful of clogging up communication channels with a surfeit of unnecessary, extra information;

■ wide communication – if we're a team, we're all a team. Make sure the communication reaches everyone.

■ Learning from geese

It's not everyone's cup of tea but, when thinking about team dynamics, I like the old and much quoted example of the geese.

By flying in a 'v' formation they create an upward air current for each other. Each flap of the wings creates uplift for the bird behind, providing 71 per cent greater flying range than if one bird flew alone.

If the leader at the front gets tired, another goose swaps place.

If a goose is sick or wounded, two others will follow it to give help and protection until they are all able to fly again.

The geese at the back do all the honking to encourage those up front to keep going

A natural example of teamwork in action.

Bibliography

Arendt, H. (1954) 'What is Authority' in H. Arendt *Between Past and Future*. New York: Viking.

Belbin, R.M. (1993) *Team Roles at Work*. Oxford: Heinemann.

Benton, D.A. (1994) *Lions Don't Need to Roar*. New York: Warner.

Birkinshaw, J. and Crainer, S. (2002) *Leadership the Sven-Goran Eriksson Way: How to Turn Your Team into Winners*. Oxford: Capstone.

Blanchard, K. (2004) *The One Minute Manager Builds High Performing Teams*. London: Harper Collins.

Boyzatis, R., Howard, A., Kapisara, B. and Taylor, G. (2004) 'Target Practice', *Harvard Business Review*, 11 March 2004.

Brighouse, T. and Woods, D. (1999) *How to Improve your School*. London: Routledge.

Cambourne, B. (1988) *The Whole Story: Natural Learning and the Acquisition of Literacy in the Classroom*. Auckland, N.Z.: Scholastic.

Casey, D. (1993) *Managing Learning in Organisations*. Buckingham: Open University Press.

Covey, S. (1989) *The 7 Habits of Highly Effective People*. London: Simon and Schuster.

Davies, B. and Ellison, L. (1999) *Strategic Direction and Development of the School*. London: Routledge.

Fullan, M. (2001) *Leading in a Culture of Change.* San Francisco: Jossey-Bass.

Gardner, H. (1996) *Leading Minds: An Anatomy of Leadership.* London: Harper Collins.

Gibson, C. and Zellmer-Bruhn, M. (2001) 'Metaphors and Meaning: An Intercultural Analysis of the Concept of Teamwork', *Administrative Science Quarterly,* 46.

Gillen, T. (2002) *Leadership Skills for Boosting Performance.* London: CIPD.

Goleman, D. (2000) 'Leadership that gets Results', *Harvard Business Review,* March–April 2000.

Handy, C. (1976) *Understanding Organisations.* London: Penguin.

Handy, C. and Aitken, R. (1986) *Understanding Schools as Organisations.* London: Pelican.

Harris, R. Baine (1976) *Authority: A Symposium.* Alabama: University of Alabama Press.

Heller, R. and Hindle, T. (1998) *Essential Manager's Manual.* London: Dorling Kindersley.

Holmes, G. (1999) *Your Conversation or Mine.* Derbyshire: Godfrey Holmes.

Landsberg, M. (1996) *The Tao of Coaching.* London: Profile.

Law, S. and Glover, D. (2000) *Educational Leadership and Learning: Practice, Policy and Research.* Buckingham: Open University.

Leigh, A. and Maynard, M. (1996) *Perfect Leader.* London: Random House.

McLeod, F. and Thomson, R. (2002) *Non Stop Creativity and Innovation: How to generate and implement winning ideas.* Maidenhead: McGraw-Hill.

Megginson, D. and Clutterbuck, D. (2005) *Techniques for Coaching and Mentoring.* Oxford: Elsevier Butterworth-Heinemann.

Moos, L., Mahony, P. and Reeves, J. (1998) 'What Teachers, Parents, Governors and Pupils Want from their Heads' in MacBeath, J. (1998) *Effective School Leadership: Responding to Change.* London: Paul Chapman.

Ofsted (2003) *Leadership and Management: What Inspection Tells Us.* London: Ofsted.

Owen, H., Hodgson, V. and Gazzard, N. (2004) *The Leadership Manual.* Harlow: Pearson.

Parsloe, T. (1995) *The Manager as Coach and Mentor.* London: Chartered Institute of Personnel and Development.

Phillips, B. (1993) *Phillips' Book of Great Thoughts and Funny Sayings.* Illinois: Tynedate.

Sergiovanni, T. (1987) *The Principalship: A Reflective Practice Perspective* (2nd edn). Boston: Allyn and Bacon.

Sergiovanni, T. (2001) *Leadership: What's in it for Schools?* London: Routledge Falmer.

Taffinder, P. (2000) *The Leadership Crash Course.* London: Kogan Page.

Tuckman, B.W. (1965) 'Developmental Sequences in Small Groups', *Psychological Bulletin,* 63(6).

Index